THE ULTIMATE ANIMAL LIBRARY

Komodo Dragons

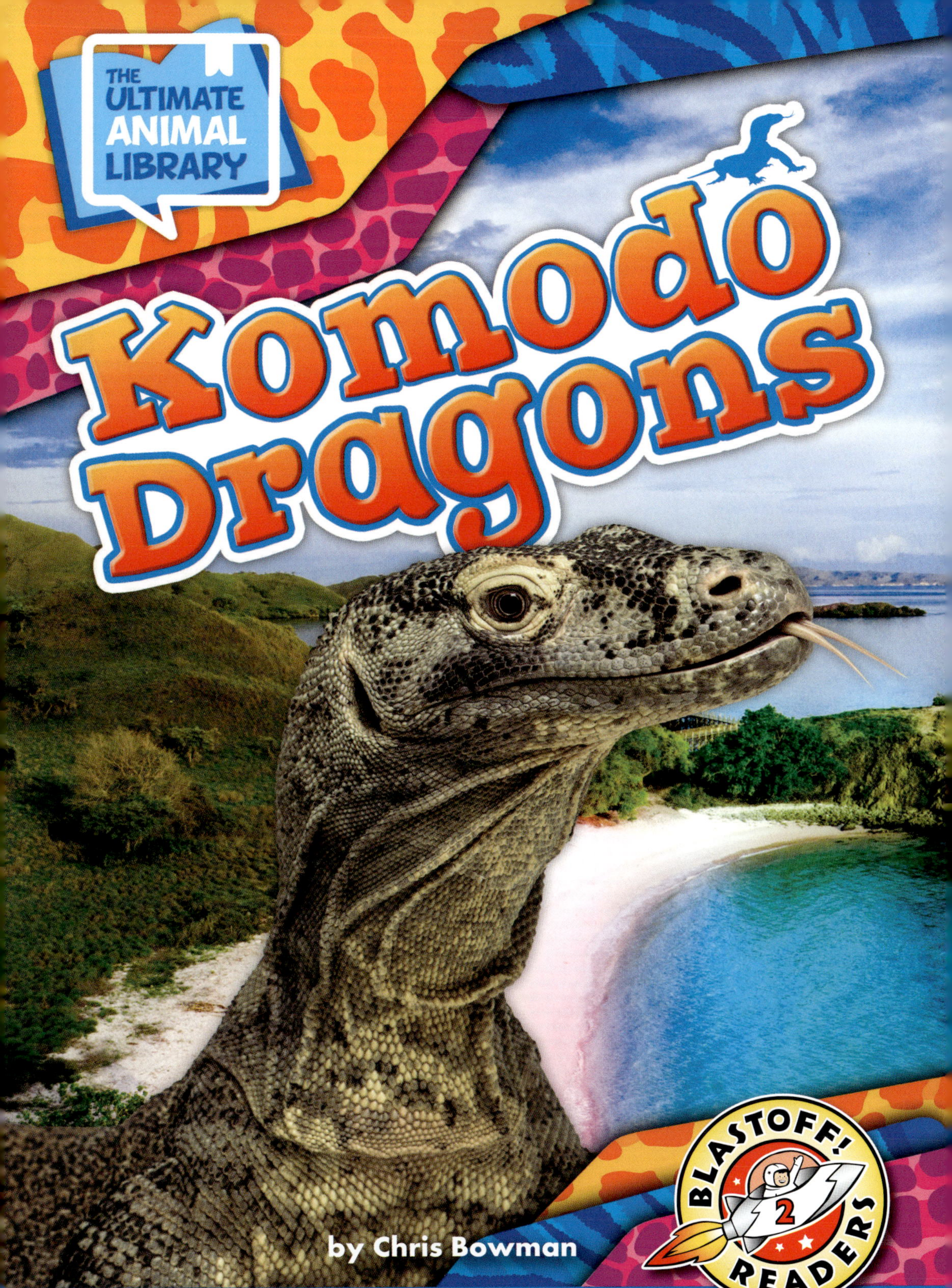

by Chris Bowman

BLASTOFF! READERS 2

BELLWETHER MEDIA • MINNEAPOLIS, MN

Blastoff! Readers are carefully developed by literacy experts to build reading stamina and move students toward fluency by combining standards-based content with developmentally appropriate text.

Level 1 provides the most support through repetition of high-frequency words, light text, predictable sentence patterns, and strong visual support.

Level 2 offers early readers a bit more challenge through varied sentences, increased text load, and text-supportive special features.

Level 3 advances early-fluent readers toward fluency through increased text load, less reliance on photos, advancing concepts, longer sentences, and more complex special features.

★ **Blastoff! Universe**

Reading Level

Blastoff! Beginners — Grade K

Blastoff! Readers — Grades 1–3

Blastoff! Discovery — Grade 4

This edition first published in 2026 by Bellwether Media, Inc.

Library of Congress Cataloging-in-Publication Data

LC record for Komodo Dragons available at: https://lccn.loc.gov/2025003962

Editor: Elizabeth Neuenfeldt Series Designer: Veah Demmin

Printed in the United States of America, North Mankato, MN.

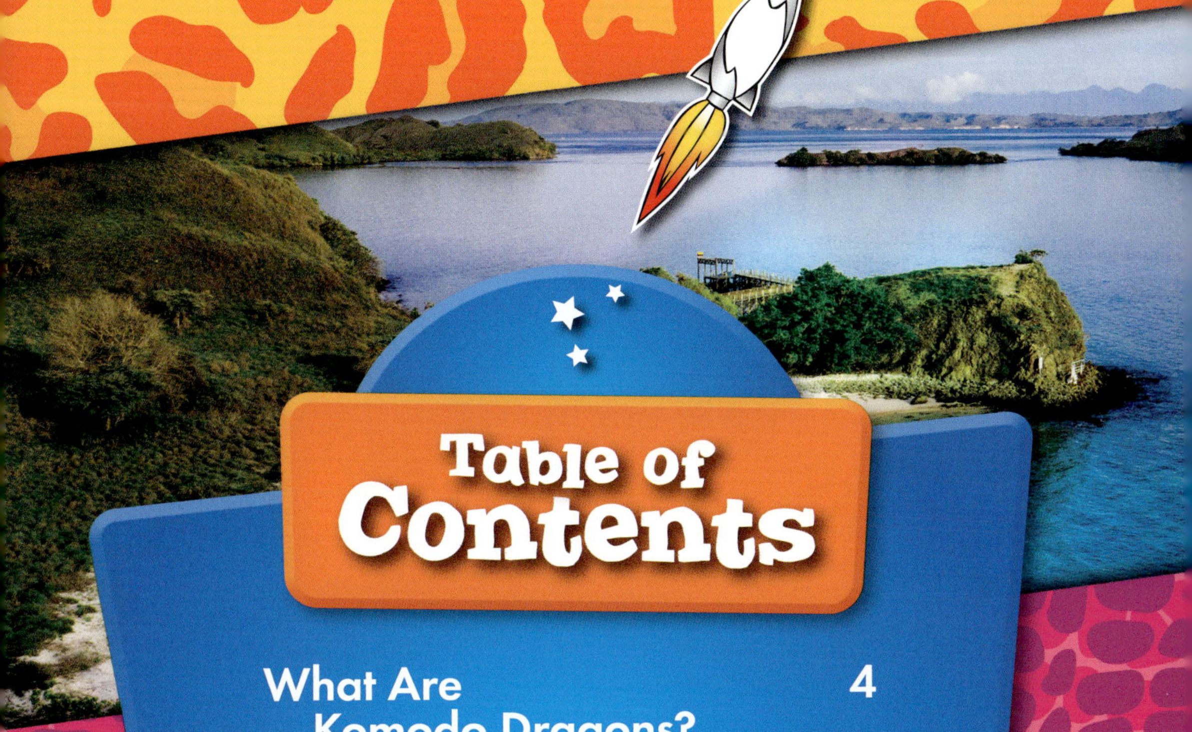

Table of Contents

What Are Komodo Dragons?

Komodo dragons are the largest lizards in the world. They can be more than 10 feet (3 meters) long! These **reptiles** live on a few islands in Indonesia.

Komodo Dragon Report

Range

Status in the Wild

Habitats

Komodo dragons are covered in **scales**. They are usually black or gray.

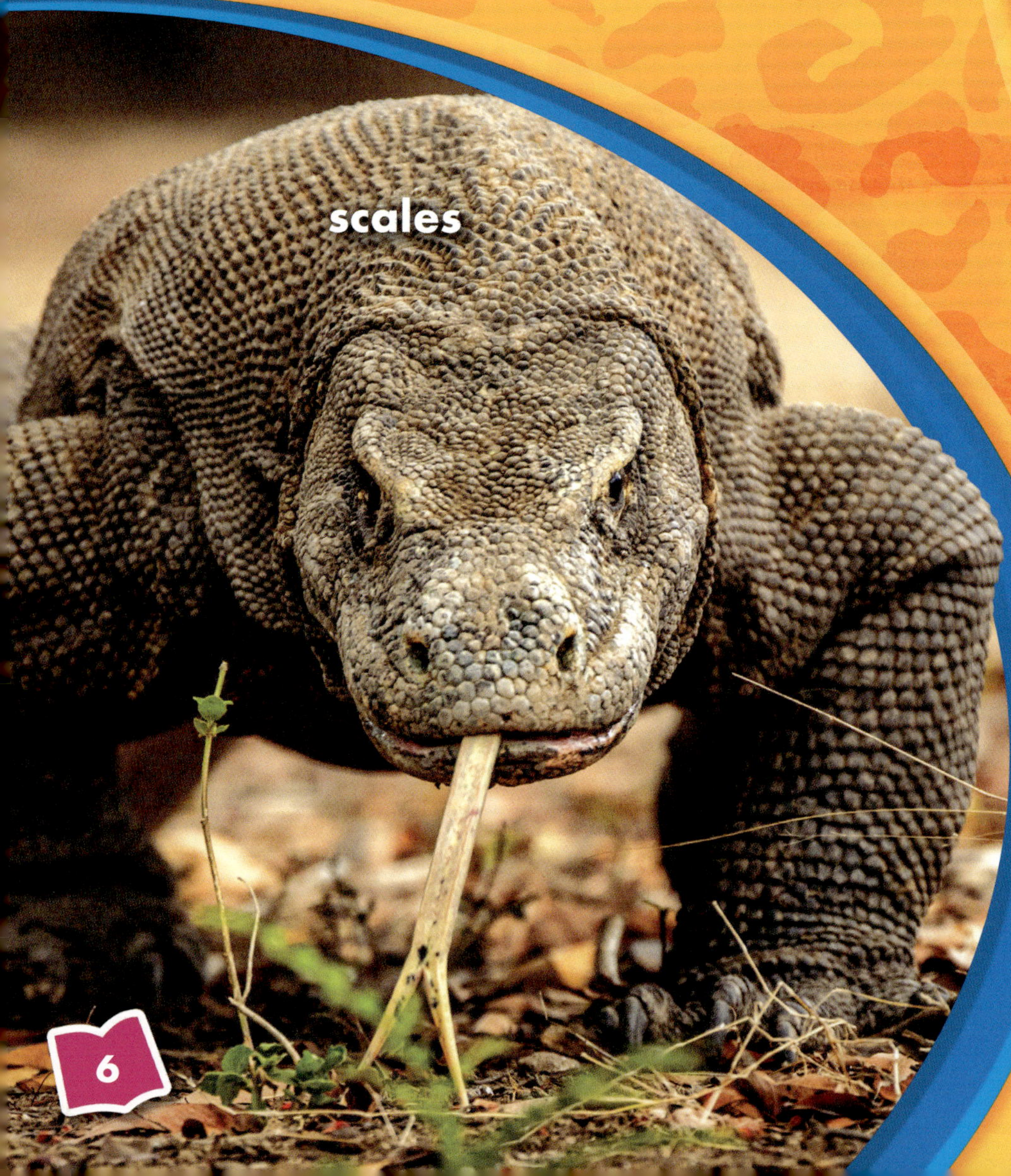

Their colors help them hide
as they hunt.

Komodos have thick necks. Their heads are long and flat. They use their **forked** tongues to smell.

Their jaws open wide to eat large **prey**.

Komodo dragons have strong legs. They have sharp claws on their feet.

Their long tails help them fight.

Spot a Komodo Dragon

Deadly Dragons

Komodo dragons live in **grasslands** and **tropical forests**. They are also found on beaches.

They rest in small **burrows** at night and during the heat of the day.

These lizards are **carnivores**. They hunt large prey such as deer and wild boars.

They also eat **carrion**.

Komodos hunt by waiting in one spot. They attack prey when it is near. They use their sharp claws and teeth.

Bacteria and **venom**
help them take down prey.

Growing Up

Female Komodo dragons lay up to 30 eggs at once. They bury the eggs in nests.

The eggs **hatch** about 9 months later. **Hatchlings** with yellow or orange stripes come out.

nest

Hatchlings live in trees to stay safe. They move to the ground when they get older.

Time to hunt
for big meals!

Life of a Komodo Dragon

Name of Babies

hatchlings

Number of Eggs

up to 30

Time Spent in Eggs

about 9 months

Life Span

up to 30 years

Glossary

bacteria—very tiny living things that can make an animal sick

burrows—tunnels or holes in the ground used as an animal's home

carnivores—animals that only eat meat

carrion—the rotting meat of a dead animal

forked—split into two parts

grasslands—lands covered with grasses and other soft plants with few bushes or trees

hatch—to break out of an egg

hatchlings—baby Komodo dragons

prey—animals that are hunted by other animals for food

reptiles—cold-blooded animals that have backbones and lay eggs

scales—plates that cover an animal's body

tropical forests—forests that have a lot of water in the air and are hot year-round

venom—poison produced by an animal, usually for hunting

To Learn More

AT THE LIBRARY

Anderson, Shannon. *Indonesia*. Minneapolis, Minn.: Bellwether Media, 2024.

Golusky, Jackie. *Komodo Dragons: Nature's Biggest Lizard*. Minneapolis, Minn.: Lerner Publications, 2024.

Grack, Rachel. *Komodo Dragons*. Minneapolis, Minn.: Bellwether Media, 2024.

ON THE WEB

FACTSURFER

Factsurfer.com gives you a safe, fun way to find more information.

1. Go to www.factsurfer.com.
2. Enter "Komodo dragons" into the search box and click .
3. Select your book cover to see a list of related content.

Index

The images in this book are reproduced through the courtesy of: Eric Isselee, cover (Komodo dragon); Petr Tran, cover background, interior background; Hendrafhx, cover (Komodo dragon icon); Eric Isselée, pp. 3, 11, 23; gudkovandrey, pp. 4, 14-15; Tai, p. 6; EinBlick, p. 7; Pitokung, p. 8; Andi K, p. 9; LifeGemz, p. 10; Uryadnikov Sergey, pp. 10-11, 16, 17; egar, p. 12; Terry Allen/ Alamy, p. 13; Longjourneys, p. 15 (deer); Hodossy, p. 15 (wild boar); Haithem, p. 15 (Komodo dragon); alfredhofer, p. 15 (carrion); Frank/ Flickr, p. 18; Nature Picture Library/ Alamy, pp. 18-19, 20; Walter Milanesi, p. 21.